To Tiffany Holmes
Warmest R
Doris Chase

ASTROLOGY AS A BUSINESS

Organization, Promotion, Handling

By

Doris Chase Doane

Published by
The American Federation of Astrologers, Inc.
P.O. Box 22040
Tempe, Arizona 85282

Books by Doris Chase Doane

Accurate World Horoscopes
Astrologers Question Box
Astrology as a Business
Astrology Rulerships
Astrology—Thirty Years Research
Contest Charts
Doane's 1981-1985 World Wide Time Change Update
Horoscopes of the U.S. Presidents
How to Prepare and Pass an Astrologer's Certificate Exam
How to Read Cosmodynes
Index to the Brotherhood of Light Lessons
Progressions in Action
Tarot Card Spread Reader (With King Keyes)
Time Changes in Canada and Mexico
Time Changes in the World
Time Changes in the USA
Vocational Selection and Counseling Vol. I and II
Zodiac: Key to Career (With C. Peel)

First Printing 1986
ISBN Number: 0-86690-303-8
Library of Congress Catalog Card Number: 85-73309

Cover Design: Lynda Kay Fullerton

Published by:
American Federation of Astrologers, Inc.
P.O. Box 22040, 6535 South Rural Road
Tempe, Arizona 85282

Printed in the United States of America

CONTENTS

ASTROLOGER

Prepares and analyzes horoscopes to advice clients regarding future events and trends. Prepares horoscope by computing position of planets, their relationship to each other and to zodiacal signs, based on factors, such as time and place subject was born. Analyzes horoscope chart to advise client, such as person or company, regarding conditions which lie ahead, course of action to follow, and probability of success or failure of that action.

DICTIONARY OF OCCUPATIONAL TERMS
U.S. Department of Labor, 1977

PREFACE

The importance of occupational information in the field of astrology cannot be stressed enough. This book offers some information that will help in providing young students as well as beginning professionals with the know-how needed to benefit from opportunities in this expanding field. Due to the rapid economical and technological changes in present day society, it is necessary to identify and study not only the skills but the environment which may affect the growth or lack of it—the composition—of a successful and rewarding astrology practice.

In addition to day-by-day operations, and aptitudes and training needed, as well as all-important public relations, this information is based on fifty years of personal experience and interviews with many astrologers, some successful and some failures from a strictly business viewpoint.

The basic purpose of this book is to present a concise and clear picture of both the tangible and intangible factors associated or involved with the astrological counselor. To be certain of attracting success in applying these suggestions, an astrologer should not overlook individual differences. Rather, he should view these recommendations in relation to the pertinent details of his client's need or his particular work attitude.

In the interest of clarity and efficiency, he should feel free to depart from rigid outlines and bend with the winds of change. However, he must be certain that any departure will contribute to the quality of his work. The proper use of these concepts make possible a work ethic of high quality to provide a maximum value of the astrologer to the community in which he serves.

Look Before You Leap

A few years back one of my former students who had become a professional asked for my advice, unfortunately after the fact. She had been practicing doing charts for friends and relatives for free for several years. She wanted to go professional and so decided to move to a large city.

Leaving her small hometown, she bought a house in the city. She uprooted her entire life and moved lock, stock and barrel bacause she thought the new location would be more open for the astrology business. But she had not been there too long before she learned that astrologers came under fortune tellers law and that her astrological practice was prohibited.

She had an idea that she could get around the law by taking and passing a professional astrologers' certificate examination, such as those held by the American Federation of Astrologers, Inc., or Professional Astrologers Incorporated.

After passing the exams with flying colors, she applied for an ad in the yellow pages of the phone book. She was told that before she could advertise there she had to have a business phone, and before she was entitled to get a business phone she had to hold a business license.

As the deadline for printing the yellow pages was critically near, she applied for a business license immediately. Then she held her breath! "Will I or won't I get it?" Was she surprised when it was issued without any question!

Throughout all the "craziness" as she called it, she had forgotten to check for zoning regulations. When she found this out, it was only two short days of having a business phone line installed in her home.

Phoning city hall to check the zoning regulation, she was utterly shocked to learn that not only was her neighborhood zoned strictly residential, but only doctors, lawyers and accountants were permitted to operate there. Professionals, but not astrologers!

She promptly called the zoning office to ask why she had received her business license if they were so strict about the zoning. The answer came that the two departments were in the process of merging because of just such a problem. She was also reminded that because of the merger her license would be revoked when she reapplied for another one at the end of the year.

By then she had not decided whether to fight the regulation or not. When she phoned the home owners association about it, she learned that they would fight a zoning change which would lower their property values.

Dazed and depressed she stewed over her problem to which there seemed no answer. Finally, she threw up her hands and started to consider relocation to a place where she could legally concentrate on her craft. Of course, this meant not only selling the house but packing up and moving again. The expense was not small!

Her story certainly illustrates the importance of looking before you leap. To fill that need, this book offers necessary steps to consider before you start an astrology business, as well as suggestions for attracting success after you decide to take that major professional plunge.

1 FACING UP TO IT

Astrology is a complex subject just as individuals are complex entities. Practicing the art and science of astrology demands much more than a cursory knowledge of the symbols in the birth chart. Handling the personal problems and the immense variety of questions from clients through counseling rests upon your expertise to interpret progressions and transits as they relate to a natal horoscope.

In addition, counseling may be enhanced by utilizing one or more branches of astrology to expend the potential seen in the birth chart. Horary astrology can be employed to answer quick questions, especially for clients who do not know their exact birth hour, or to explain and pinpoint multiple energy releases indicated in the natal chart. A horary question often defines into which department of life the abundant energy is likely to flow.

Then electional astrology embraces factors allowing the selection of propitious times to take action, such as the opening of a business, a job chart, a marriage chart, founding a business cooperation, expanding an operation or a merger, and the like.

Synastry (chart comparison) is another effective branch of astrology. It can be employed to compare the potentials and reactions of individuals in all types of human relationships, such as families, friends, clients, lawyers, accountants, employee/employer, etc. These people are often important to the progress of the person, business or vocation your client is involved with.

Another branch is called mundane astrology, dealing with world affairs. Delineating these mundane charts reveals trends concerning the political, economic and mass psychological environment in which the client is functioning at any given period.

In today's society where physical fitness is all the rage, we see signs of a striving for mental fitness. Clients are seeking to build up a positive, spiritual attitude, in order to attract more happiness, satisfaction and a sense of usefulness into their life styles. Esoteric or spiritual, astrology can be applied to point up guiding indicators for these clients to pursue—programs which they can put into action that will lead them in the desired direction.

Let us assume that your astrological education in these areas has come to the point where you want to set up shop and start practicing. You are now faced with making proper preparations—the gestation period for the birth of your business. Its success will be limited only by your own imagination, interest, drive and dedication if your business is opened after certain precautions are met. This demands the consideration of legality, location, financing, marketing, promotion and keeping records.

Let us presume that by visiting city hall you have all the legal information together. You have found that it is possible to conduct an astrology business at your present location. *Pause before you take action.*

Self Examination

It is time for a little soul-searching to help you decide whether you really want to take on this responsibility. Will you gain joy and fulfillment from being a professional astrologer? The answers to the following questions will help you decide:

1. Would I enjoy a serving occupation?
2. Do I want to work with people?

3. Do I want an active, sedentary job? One that demands concentration?
4. Are my skills adequate, and can I prove it by a certificate of proficiency? If not, should I take brushup courses or advanced classes?
5. How much income do I have to make?
6. Will I do well where I live now?
7. Do I want to move before starting to practice?
8. Can I expect the cooperation of my family and friends?
9. Do I have enough financing to set up the business?

Business Demands

Also to help you make your decision, you should think through clearly the disadvantages of conducting your own business and consider what being an astrologer demands of you:

1. Working long hours (not goofing off or waiting until you are in the mood).
2. Being at the beck and call of others, sometimes 24 hours a day.
3. The necessity of keeping an objective professional approach no matter how much your emotions or health are upset. Self-control.
4. Taking constuctive measures to offset the sedentary work. (All work and no play make Jack a dull FAT boy!)
5. Taking the entire responsibility for the product you produce (no passing the buck).
6. Having the patience and perserverence to keep records right up to date and meeting deadlines. (I'll do your chart in two weeks.)
7. Not letting flattery nourish an ego trip.
8. Take criticism in an adult manner.
9. Using system and organization to eliminate wasting your valuable time.

Traps to Avoid

Do you know why 50% of all new businesses fail in the first two years? Here are reasons listed by the U.S. Department of Commerce:

1. Lack of capital.
2. Choosing the wrong business.
3. Too large a financial load (overly-high loans, debts, rents).
4. Poor location.
5. Poor judgment.
6. Lack of experience and ability.
7. Lack of salesmanship.
8. Poor record keeping.
9. Poor credit policies.

After recording your answers to these probing points of query, study them carefully. Now if your survey does not turn you off, you are ready to proceed with the analysis and consideration of the many business subjects you will be forced to face.

2 EDUCATION

Both the environment and the legal aspect of conducting a business are of prime importance to the successful astrological practice. However, education and training in astrology are at the base of the profession. After all, one can always move to another location where the environment and the laws are more conducive to an astrological practice. But you cannot engage in successful counseling until you have received an adequate education.

Merely reading astrology textbooks, no matter how many of them, cannot and will not educate the neophyte to go on to become a professional counselor. Rather, a solid educational background is required. That is difficult to come by in some areas. However, correspondence courses can furnish help in readying for the certificate exams that speak of your expertise.

It goes without saying that an academic education is important—no less than a high school diploma. Even better is a college degree in psychology and a minor in sociology and economics.

Why? It is true that many college courses are time consuming and unproductive, but astrology can be associated with everything in the universe. The more the astrologer is familiar with man and all of his relations with his environment, the more competent practitioner that astrologer is apt to become.

Another fact of an all-round education which embraces man, his actions and his environment is reading—all kinds of information from magazines, book, journals and the like which deal with news, health, business trends, social studies and other related topics.

As I wrote that, it brought to mind an experience my husband, John Lawson Ahern, had back in the 1960s. Being a Gemini he reads everything he can get his hands on. Who would think that he would be able to help his clients because he had read a Scottish medical journal?

These particular clients, a couple from a very hot area of California, came to him as a last resort. They wanted children. Although they had a child a year or so after they married, for the past ten years they had not conceived. Visiting one doctor after another and having tons of expensive tests performed had not helped. They were told that there was no medical reason why they should not have more children.

When he looked at the charts while talking to the wife, he came to the conclusion that she was not the problem. Just the opposite, because she had an extremely fertile chart. The husband, however, had a fire sign rising on the Ascendant of his natal chart with Venus in exact conjunction to that Ascendant. Venus ruled the cusp of the fifth house of children. Natal Mars was located in his twelfth house and had progressed up to the conjunction aspect of the Venus-Ascendant combination.

John thought, "He's too hot!" Then that medical report he had read sprang to his mind. That research had proved that a cause of male infertility was wearing jockey shorts because they kept the testicles up tight against the scrotum and therefore too hot, which affected the sperm mobility. Due to the fact that her husband worked outside in the extreme heat, she was asked, "What kind of shorts does he wear?"

Looking rather surprised, the wife answered, "Jockey shorts."

That was the problem. Once he switched to boxers and consciously tried to stay cooler, she became pregnant in slightly over six months. At last count, they had had three more children.

Heat affecting sperm mobility was little known in the 1960s. Yet John's casual reading had prepared him with this information that provided helpful counsel for a client.

Being well read in all phases of life is a must for a busy, practicing astrologer. How can we counsel on business and finances for instance if we never read about them in the newspapers and journals? We realize that we cannot act as a financial advisor, but this information can help us to understand the economical environment as it relates to other departments of life. Limiting ourselves to astrological texts may enhance our technical ability, but it does not do much to increase the effectiveness of dealing with everyday problems.

There is no question about it. At the present time astrological education leaves something to be desired. Many of the so-called schools of astrology entertain rather than educate. In others, the curriculum is inadequate, often stopping at the primary level where the student acquires a bunch of keywords. He is left wondering what to do next, for he has no idea of how to synthesize these words except in a choppy way often resulting in glaring contradictions.

In light of this, each neophyte should insure that he will gain the all-encompassing knowledge he needs from private tutors or class sessions conducted by astrologers who are certified. Perhaps the most profitable step is to write to two different organizations requesting information about competent astrological educators in your area as well as those who handle correspondence courses through the mail. The addresses are:

The American Federation of Astrologers, Inc. (AFA)
P.O. Box 22040
Tempe, Arizona 85282

Professional Astrologers Incorporated (PAI)
4606 Earl Lane
Santa Maria, California 93455

After the listing from each arrives, send for the information. Study the literature carefully when it is returned to you. If possible, discuss your choices with a professional astrologer. Then make your choice. It is wise to choose one who is certified. All of those from PAI are professional. The AFA has two grades: one is the student level which is signified by AMAFA and the professional certified astrologer who uses the letters PMAFA (Professional Member American Federation of Astrologers, Inc.)

Astrology is a complex study. Therefore it is self-defeating to begin a course unless you will be able to stick with it without goofing off. Constant study application is required until natal astrology is mastered in its fundamentals. After that, it is possible to take your time about branching out into other areas. That is because natal astrology contains some of the elements of all other branches of astrology.

3 BASIC TRAINING

If possible you should attend a school of astrology run by people who are certified professionals. If there are none available in your area, then contact an accredited astrologer who offers a correspondence course in standard astrology. It is true that while most of our studies are done by ourselves, having a teacher is invaluable for two reasons. In the first place you cannot just take it for granted that you know some aspect of the subject. You have to prove that you know the answers to the assignment because your lessons are corrected by an expert.

In addition, the very subject of astrology itself raises many questions in your mind as you progress through the various levels of understanding. After all, astrology can be associated with everything in the universe. Your questions can be answered by your teacher, and if he does not know them he can refer you to someone who can.

As you proceed through the first lessons that you receive, there is much you can do to progress rapidly in your studies. That invaluable help is based upon repetition. Not only will it assist in speeding up and developing your expertise, it will shorten your time considerably to apprenticeship.

The material upon which you can apply this repetition is the birth data—date, place and hour—of your close friends and relatives. Sometimes this is difficult to do, especially finding the exact birth hour. To be sure that this datum is correct, ask the person to get a copy of his birth registration for you. The hour of birth may be written on the certificate. Explain to him the difference between a birth certificate and a birth registration. (See Chapter 12)

Now it is time to take your first professional step forward. Start a file folder for each person. Place the birth information into the appropriate files. Then, as you learn the steps in chart erection, calculate each problem on each of the accumulated birth data. Later on, you can also figure each mathematical step of the progressions as your assignments come along.

How many charts? Twelve charts is a good round number to start with. Too few charts would not give the repetition necessary to learn each math step. On the other hand, working with too many charts could cause discouragement. It is also important to let your friends and relatives know that you are not going to give them a reading, you are just practicing.

At first, you will be occupied with learning astrological math for erecting natal charts, aspect calculation between the planets, Midheaven and Ascendant, progressions, transits and the like. To balance your studies you should also be reading books on beginning and intermediate delineation. The American Federation of Astrologers will, upon your request, send you the *Natal Astrology Directory* of the various reference books.

During this period of study you should also be occupied with gathering other information that will help you understand astrology better in the future. Start a case history on each person in your files. It will develop over a period of time, but you should keep at it—continuing to make notes of events, so that each case will be ready when you are. When the time comes, in intermediate and advanced delineation and counseling you can use these cases to test your skill in synthesizing all of the chart symbols.

This chore of writing a case history on each person will demand your utmost objectivity. Never jump to conclusions about the thoughts, feelings and actions of people. Remember, we are all actors on the stage of life and as such, we seldom reveal our deepest convictions even to our closest friends. So you will have to stay cool and become a sort of psychological sleuth to determine the factors which you will add to each case history.

Question your subject carefully before entering notations on the case history. The facts about each trait, accomplishment, wish or event in life are widely covered in the sample case history questionnaire presented in Chapter 12. It is not necessary to have all of these questions answered, but it certainly would be helpful to your study progress. Remember, also, that some people do not like to talk about themselves, while others cannot seem to stop. Be prepared to be discreet in either case.

A beneficial practice to adopt to insure a detailed case history is to keep a pad and pencil by the phone at all times. Then when a person tells you about what is happening in his life, you can jot it down. Ask intelligent questions to get proper information. Did you get hurt? Where? What time did it happen? Was anyone with you? Be sure to record the date, hour and place of the event.

Another area for your personal research is the chart of a celebrity. Their lives are well publicized, if you can believe all you read. When an outstanding event occurs in their lives, you can progress the appropriate chart to that time to see how the planets and other astrological factors were operating at the time. A splendid place to find correct birth data of celebrities is a cloumn in the *AFA Bulletin* entitled "Data Exchange," or in Lois Rodden's *Profiles of Women,* published by the AFA.

Keeping a close watch on the changing life patterns of the people in your research group will teach you more than reading thousands of books. This is not to say that book information is unimportant, but we need to advance beyond merely reading to application. Keeping the case histories up-to-date ready to read and study is one way of going forward.

After mastering one system of chart reading thoroughly, you will have fashioned a rigid ruler which can be used to test other approaches. Never stop learning and investigating. Read about all other methods and ideas, then test them in your charts. Do they really reflect the events in a person's life? Is the method helpful in expanding your technique in counseling? If not, into the round file that particular theory goes!

All of this is merely the start of your training period. But it is vital to your progress. Unfortunately, there are very few opportunities open to become an apprentice to a professional astrologer. Perhaps the next best way to gain inside information is to become an astrologer's secretary or "gofer." This will place you in an environment where you are constantly exposed to the know-how and methods important to a successful professional practice.

4 LEGAL ASPECTS AND ENVIRONMENT

Now after receiving your education and training, the next step in your progress is to obtain a proficiency certificate. Both the American Federation of Astrologers and Professional Astrologers Incorporated (mentioned earlier) hold monitored exams periodically. When you feel you are ready, write to each for information.

Many astrologers hold both certificates. When you have passed the examination successfully for either organization (or hopefully both of them) you will be awarded a certificate suitable for framing.

By all means pass both exams and then frame and hang the certificates on your office wall in a prominent place. Not only does this say that you have proven yourself thus bolstering your self-confidence, it also educates the public (your clients) to the fact that are you a competent astrologer who has an educational background and has demonstrated the fact by sitting for an eight-hour examination.

Even though these certificates have an official appearance, they do not make it legal for you to practice, no matter where you live. They merely indicate that you have demonstrated your expertise by passing the examinations.

Now you have reached the point of going into business for yourself. The laws regulating astrologers as well as the environment in which you will practice must be considered. It is imperative that before opening your door to clients, you have made this thorough investigation first lest a jail door loom in your future and/or horrendous expense extricating yourself from a situation that only required forethought and planning.

Your initial decision should be whether you will conduct your practice at home or in an office away from home. A trip to city hall will gain necessary information. There you can learn whether a business license is required and if zoning laws allow you to practice in your selected area.

Legality. Your very first priority is to find out if you will be allowed to practice astrology at all. If so, go on from there. In some areas an astrology business may be conducted without a license and without adhering to any regulation. In others it is strictly regulated. In most localities it is forbidden because the word *astrology* appears in the ordinance concerning fortune telling. In others, a person may obtain a teacher's license and treat each client as a student.

The steps of legal regulation follow this order: City or town laws are superseded by county laws, and county laws are superseded by state laws. In the last analysis, state laws are superseded by federal (national) laws.

At the present writing there are no national (federal) laws regulating astrology and its practice. Some states have a regulation on the books stating that counties or cities may enact their own ordinances which prohibit or regulate astrologers. However, at this time no state has specific laws regulating the practice of astrology.

Each town or city ordinance needs to be checked to learn if the practice of astrology is legal when clients are charged a fee. In some cases where this information has been requested, the office clerk does not appear to know anything about it. Then, the aspiring professional astrologer should ask for the ordinance outlining fortune telling (bunco), because that is where the word "astrology" often appears.

Zoning. If you plan to do business in your home, check the zoning laws with the county or city clerk. A wide variance is found from one location to another. In some, you are allowed to conduct a home business provided no customers come to your home (service is given by mail or phone). Certain city regulations state that small business in residential neighborhoods must have an assessed property value of not less than a stated number of dollars. Others allow practice only in a business office and not at home in a residential area. Each city or town has its own regulations which change from time to time.

Licenses. In some business localities no business license is needed for a home business. In others, the annual fee varies widely. It may be strictly forbidden, or a license may be obtained after a certain period of residency.

Let us assume that after checking with city hall you find that you will be allowed to practice astrology under a business license either in your home or in an office downtown. At this point you need to consider the resistance of the physical environment. I am sure you will agree that computers would not sell well to a primitive African tribe, nor would bikini sales be very brisk at the North Pole. Neither environment would provide a successful outlet for those products.

So you need to be aware of the type of clients you hope to attract as well as their needs. Some astrologers specialize. They serve clients with marital or family problems, others handle clients who need to make business decisions, etc.

For instance, creating a professional atmosphere into which business clients come would hardly be possible if it were located next to a popular playground crowded with squealing children. Selecting the appropriate environment in which to give your consultations is as significant as an area where a specific type of client finds easy and comfortable access.

Location. When selecting a location for your business, check out the supply and demand as well as the competition in the area. Of course, if you handle your practice through the mail, these physical conditions need not be considered, except perhaps the proximity of the post office and the parking situation in that vicinity. By mail, your clients contact you through a box number.

In a mail business you are protected legally as long as you do not use the mails to defraud or advertise falsely. Producing what you have promised to do and conducting your business within a reasonable length of time will allow you to meet the legal regulations of a mail order business. A post office mandate demands that mail orders be filled within thirty days of their receipt.

As long as we are concerned with the legal aspect of practicing astrology at this point, it may not be out of place to discuss the release which the client should sign before each business transaction. This is just another step you can take to protect yourself. The following release is one that I use. You may wish to reword it to reflect your own personality. If so, be sure your version presents a clearcut explanation of the fact that you are not telling your client's fortune.

I hereby request you to inform me concerning the planetary forces active on the date of my birth and at other times during my life, the dates of which I will give you. I affirm that these are the true dates to the best of my knowledge.

In furnishing me this information, I understand that you obtained it from charts constructed by you, and from textbooks covering the art/science of astrology and astronomy.

I understand that you make no claim to any special or occult power and that the information you will furnish will be only that which any thorough student of astrology would give me.

I understand that I am not asking you to tell my fortune in any sense, nor do I understand that you attempt or pretend to do so.

Name______________________________ Date________

Address______________________ Telephone____________

Signature______________________________

Turn to Chapter 12 to see how this release form was effectively modified by one of my colleagues to see how he projected his own personality.

Because most of our clients do not understand astrological terminology, we should ask them if they want it included in their reading. If they do not, there will be more time and space to amplify on the matters that are of specific concern to their personal interests. After all, it is not too informative to tell a client he has Jupiter square Mars if he hasn't the foggiest notion of what Jupiter, Mars or a square stands for.

To handle this effectively, add a question at the end of the release form to read: *If you are familiar with astrology, do you wish me to include astrological terms in your analysis?* ☐ *Yes* ☐ *No.*

Applying the precautions of having a signed release and avoiding predictions act as insurance against an accusation of breaking the law.

5 FINANCES

Many professional astrologers have started out by serving friends and relatives, usually for no fee. By doing this for a few years, they learn their craft and hone their abilities. At the time they are ready to become practicing professionals, see clients and charge for their services, as a rule they have also passed at least one proficiency exam.

If you are a beginner, you should think about that. Before rushing into the project of establishing an astrology business, it is to your advantage to become aware of the financial picture. Because it takes considerable time to build up a clientele whose fees will support such a business, it is wise to stash away at least 18 months' living expenses in the bank before quitting a job in another field. A well-clothed, housed, and fed astrologer does a better job counseling.

Then before practicing full time, it might even be wise for you to work at a part-time job. This could relieve a lot of anxiety while you are establishing your practice until your name and services become known in your community.

Remember, if you have a solid source of income—even from a part-time job—it really helps to ease the fear of starting up and sustaining a small business—a serious responsibility.

Some of these steps may seem like a slow beginning, especially to one who is looking forward to serving mankind or becoming his own boss. But a small start (unless there is plenty of capital available) allows ease of living and ample time to build up essentials to the craft.

The Wall Street Journal points out that in addition to inexperience and incompetence, taking unwarranted risks and speculation with finances are the main causes for small business failure.

There are several financial angles that the would-be independent entrepreneur should study. Understandably, the basic financial requirement after paying for an education (including course tuition and the cost of books and supplies) is the capital to fund your practice. At the start when you set up your business checking account (or even before if the opportunity becomes available) you should enter into a friendly relationship with the bank personnel. It won't be long before you will be able to have conversations with one of the officers of the bank.

Then when you are ready to borrow money for your business, you can initiate or expand a relationship where you can feel confident about interviewing your "friend." He will advise you of the many different plans the bank offers when making loans as well as describe the collateral required. You will need to provide financial statements which are described later.

Nothing can take the place of a personal relationship within your bank. In fact, even if you are beginning a new account in a bank and applying for a loan at the same time, NEVER walk in off the street and ask to see someone. That alone proves you are a neophyte in business procedures and is not at all conducive to getting the bank's cooperation.

Telephone beforehand and find out who the head loan officer is. Then make an appointment to see him.

When you arrive for that appointment, be certain you conform to accepted norms of business dress, hairstyle and deportment. All of us like to be independent, and some want to dress in the heights or depths of fashion. But when you are trying to impress a banker is definitely not the time to assert your personal idiosyncrasies.

When you arrive, have all of your information neatly arranged. It should include:

1. Back income tax records.
2. Personal resume and financial statement.

3. Outline of business you are beginning and anticipated income and expenses.
4. Original deposit.

One of the first things business experts emphasize when they tell about becoming successful is to develop a head for figures and keeping records. Fortunately, the very nature of the astrologer's preparatory work encourages the development of knowledge in both of these areas.

Once the business is started, these techniques support a smooth running operation if applied consistently. Income and expenditure records should be kept up-to-date so that when you assemble your tax information to give to your accountant at the end of the year the job will not become a headache. When the business expands enough, a home computer can do a quick, neat job on these items.

One of the best ways to keep track of expenses is to open a separate business checking account. Start with at least $100.00 (but you will do better to hike that to $500.00). Pay as many bills as possible with a check or use credit cards so that you will have a record of every expenditure. If you have to spend cash for those little incidentals that are associated with this work, be sure to ask for a sales slip at the time of purchase as proof of the expenditure.

You can keep these incidental sales slips for a month or so, then total them with a breakdown of the different type items as well as the check number and date. It will read something like this:

Copies	$ 2.85
Postage	6.13
Supplies	8.31
UPS	2.72
	20.01

pd 6/8/82 #7838

Rent

Whether you do your work in an office or in an area in your own home, you must keep track of the rent you pay.

If you rent a regular business office, the process is clearcut. But if you plan to conduct your business at home, adhere to the ground rules.

Familiarize yourself with the IRS regulations dealing with business conducted where you live. These regulations change from year to year. Also, it is a good idea to take black and white snapshots from all directions inside your office, making sure that your equipment, files, typewriter, computer, word processor and so forth are easily recognized. Keep these on file with your income tax records.

As a rule rent depends upon the percentage of the home area used to conduct your business. Broadly, a certain percentage of your rent, mortgage payment, or whatever usually can be taken as rent for your business. These guidelines are changeable and sometimes not easily defined. Consult your accountant at the end of the year when you give him the entire total rent you have paid in that year. He can then deduct the allowable percentage from the total rent if your office is in your home.

In 1983 new regulations released by the IRS seemed to be more lenient for people working out of their homes. Life styles have introduced a new element into the home office place.

Many more people are now using home computers to do their work. Even though your deductions are still limited to the amount of your business income in that part of the home, it is no longer necessary to set up a separate room in your house to be used exclusively for the business. Your accountant can explain this change among others.

Stationery, Letterheads

Notice the statements of your doctor, lawyer, accountant. Do they appear on paper with lots of symbols, birds, flowers, wheels, colors and so forth decorating the edges? Hardly! Usually they are executed on a computer on plain white paper. Do your statements and letterheads, etc., use a dignified conservative logo, if you cannot restrain yourself? The color and quality of the paper is important. What we are seeking in this area is the professional look.

The composition of your statement is another area where you can adopt the professional look. When you are charged with an office call by your doctor, you are presented with a bill to cover the ordinary expenses of an examination and consultation. For instance, his bill does not list the price of each item used in the examination, such as 10¢ for a cotton swab, 15¢ for a tongue depressor, $3.50 for a blood pressure check, or a fee for taking your vital signs—temperature, pulse and respiration.

Fees for Service

These might include prices for several different types of counseling work, such as a natal reading, a horary chart, a chart comparision (synastry), etc., as well as phone informational readings. Many professionals establish a fee for phone calls, for either new work or follow-ups. This is especially effective with clients who own/operate businesses. They are looking for quick answers.

You should decide upon a package fee that automatically takes care of the chart blanks, cassettes, postage, or whatever. Then all you will have to include on the statement is the price of the various treatments your client ordered. Natal and progressed chart $0.00, or chart comparison $0.00. The statement can be refined even more to look professional in the following manner:

For professional service   Due $000.00

In each of these areas make sure your price structure is high enough to cover all of your costs plus a decent return for your efforts and investment. Underpricing is a prime cause of business failure.

Overhead Expenses

One of your most important expenses will be paying your accountant. Be sure he is one who keeps abreast of the changes in the tax laws that occur from time to time.

One record you will be called upon to keep is that of taxes. Among them will be federal taxes, state taxes, sales taxes, etc. So you can see that there are many ramifications to running your own business. How true is that old saw, "You have to spend money to make money."

Start at the very beginning to be neat and orderly. That will prevent headaches and stress along the line when you are surrounded by piles of paper from which you will gather pertinent information.

In order to prevent confusion you will need to keep accurate records of every business related item, no matter how small. Make sure that all expenses are backed up by a receipt of purchase.

Say, you buy some liquid paper at the stationers store or have several copies made at the printers. You pay cash. Then insist upon a sales slip.

Of course this means there will be numerous slips of paper involved. Not to worry! Pay them as we have mentioned earlier. Take an expanding file folder, which gives you sections for the twelve months of the year. Insert receipt bank statements and canceled checks with their bank statements into the proper date partitions.

Another item to include in the expanding file folder is the bank deposit slip (always keep a copy for yourself). For quick reference, on your copy of the deposit slip, be sure to itemize what each amount stands for as far as income is concerned. If there is scant room on the deposit slip for words, then you can use numbers as a code. Write in colored ink, 3 for consultation, 4 for articles sold, 5 for book royalties, 6 for lecture fees. Most important, keep all of these records up to date and neatly filed in their proper places.

Now all of the material for both income and expense is readily available by months. At the end of the year it will be a simple matter to verify anything in the information to go to your accountant that seems questionable to him. You can look it up in short order.

The list you make out for your accountant should include the following items:

Supplies: Computerized math work from an outside service, software, stationery, letterheads, business cards, envelopes, mailing envelopes, pens, pencils, writing materials, carbon paper, address labels, machine rentals and the like.

Advertising: Telephone listing, birthday and Christmas cards, ad space in organizational programs, magazines, journals, newspapers, books given gratis for endorsements, reviews, etc., flyers describing you and the services you offer.

Dues and subscriptions: Expenses undertaken to maintain or improve your professional skills. Dues to astrology organizations (such as PAI or AFA), educational expenses such as for workshops, seminars, conferences, etc., business related club dues, subscriptions to journals, magazines and other print media. University or school expenses associated with business.

Travel: Keep a record of travel expenses, meal, lodging, books, supplies when you travel to attend a conference or when you conduct a workshop.

Taxes: Federal, state, sales, etc.

Insurance:

Postage: Mailing or private carrier postage. Be sure to get a slip at the post office when you buy stamps or even mail just one package.

Telephone: If a personal phone is used, ask accountant to take allowable percentage of regular charges, then check long distance and record those for business.

Utilities: Lights, heat, water.

Maintenance: Janitorial service, garbage pickup, trips to dump or anything done to maintain business property. Consult accountant if work is done by the hour.

Miscellaneous: Covers any and all items not categorized, such as repairs, loss, damage through casualty.

Contributions: Any donation to an incorporated non-profit body (like the AFA or PAI, etc.) is considered a charitable organization. Once a year it is a good idea to check about your office to see if you can donate furniture, equipment or other items no longer used to a charitable organization (such as the Salvation Army, Good Will, etc.). You are allowed a certain percentage of the total worth as a tax writeoff. Be sure to get a receipt for any of these transactions. It goes without saying that your donation to any organization (be it a church or whatever) should be sent by check. This is a recorded expense for your files.

Depreciation of furniture and funishings: Desk, chairs, typing table, filing cabinet, lamps, rugs, curtains, etc. At the time these items are purchased, make a list (or even better make a copy) of the costs of each one. Keep them up to date, filed in a separate file for this purpose. Once your accountant writes off the first depreciation, he makes allowance for future years automatically.

Depreciation of equipment: Telephone answering machine, typewriter, computer, word processor, pencil sharpener, tape recorder, calculator, copy machine, etc. Keep the cost of these on hand as well.

Running a small business takes patience and sticking to details until a job of work is completed. Finishing your expense records once a month while these expenditures (or income, for that matter) are still fresh in your mind will assuredly ease later frustration. What about the . . .

Income

Even though it may come from various sources, income is much easier to keep track of. This may be due to the fact that many different items are not involved. As stated before, when you bank your income write on the deposit slip that you keep for yourself the source and amount of the check. Having a specific account at the bank for your business (with no personal entries) keeps the best financial record.

We have touched on many topics in this chapter. However, the important thing to remember is that a business goes under if there is mismanagement, inadequate capital or misplaced confidence. Those words may seem negative. Not so! Facing these facts and being prepared to do something about them is like raising your umbrella when you step out into the rain—an intelligent precautionary action.

Eye on the Ball

According to the actions taken to insure a successful business, the Small Business Administration offers this advice: Records in a home business need not be elaborate but you should know at any time the answers to the following:

How much business am I doing?
How much is credit business?
How much cash do I have?
How much is in inventory?
How much money do I owe?
How much gross margin did I earn?
What is my net profit?
How much tax do I pay?
How much am I worth?
Am I going up or down financially?

Daily records must show cash taken in and cash paid out. Forms for this can be purchased at any stationery store.

You also need a Profit and Loss Statement at least once a year to determine how you are doing financially. If you have kept good daily records, any accountant will figure this for a reasonable cost.

More helpful information is presented in booklets published by the Small Business Administration, U. S. Department of Commerce, Washington, D.C. 20025. Send for a list of their counseling booklets. Such informative reading may be just what you need at the present stage of your business growth to inspire your creativity to move on to better methods.

6 SETTING UP AN OFFICE

Before thinking of setting up an office—whether in a shopping mall, a business complex, or in your own home—the important thing is to measure your chances scientifically in the light of the foregoing information. Be as objective as possible in determining your competence and experience. Also make sure your credit and capital are sufficient to carry you over some rough spots.

Having decided that your own horoscope with its progressions and transits indicates a good time to start such a venture, your next step is to select an appropriate moment to begin. One thing to remember is to allow time for gestation—to do all of the things needed before you open your door to the public.

Through the trial and error charts you will be able to pick an electional figure mapping the strength/harmony in the seventh house (clients and the public in general); the sixth house (service and working conditions); and the trinity of wealth. These are the tenth house, the business and reputation as well as publicity; the second house, the business income and general financial picture; and the eighth house, the client's ability to pay, loans you may have and your relationship with your accountant.

Be sure not to overlook the first house in the electional chart. It maps not only the pyschical energy and strength, but the vitality of the business as well as yours. This is significant and should take a prominent place in your search for the right starting moment. Physical stamina is needed to withstand the long work hours as well as the sedentary atmosphere of a job that requires concentration and diligent application.

If you plan to have a practice where you come face to face with your client, make sure to schedule a consultation at the hour of the electional chart. The business should start to operate on the things it is designed to do at that moment. Also, your first customer must be a paying client in order to energize the selected chart.

If your operation is to be conducted through the mail, prepare all of your literature ahead of time. Then drop it into the mail box at the exact hour and minute of the selected chart. Immediately return to your desk and work in order to add the necessary energy.

In either case, the launching has been accomplished. Now plunge into the publicity programs you have planned from the information given in Chapter 10.

Gestation

Before you initiate your venture there are still things to be done. During this gestation period you should design the space where you will see your clients. That should be a quiet place where the door can be closed to insure privacy. Or, if you handle the interpretations through the mail, plan how you will package and mail the information to your client. Whatever way the client is served make sure the ambiance of a professional is reflected in all that you do.

Naturally, an office away from home is more professional, especially as seen by the public at large. In any case your office should be comfortable for both you, the astrologer, and your client.

Organize the furniture to make the work easy, and leave some open space for breathing. Be selective about what is placed on the walls in addition to your framed certificates of astrological proficiency.

Use soothing colors and restrained fabrics to offset a growing plant or two. But skip the smothering gypsy tearoom look of many hanging ferns and the like.

A clean, organized office reflects the image of the professional who knows what he is doing and is successful at doing it. If your desk is strewn with piles of folders and papers, you give an impression that it takes you forever to finish readings. Furthermore, such a cluttered environment will not help you to keep your own thoughts uncluttered. When a client spies such a mess on your desk, he may feel that it will take you forever to get around to doing the work for him.

Consult Chapter 8 where you will find a study of work procedures. Adopting these hints will assist you to provide your clients with a consultation place reflecting a professional air.

7 ATTITUDE AND BEHAVIOR

The Carnegie Foundation conducted a study to determine causes of success. Their findings revealed that "85% of success in business is due not to superior knowledge but to superior ability to influence others."

Personal public relations (PR)—the relation of one individual to his public (whether that public is an individual, a group, or a nation)—is extremely significant.

PR is determined by how a person acts—what he does—what he writes—what he says—and the impression he creates on other people. PR is strictly a definite, personal, crystal-clear philosophy of living. It springs from the heart, out of the mouth and into a person's actions.

When we talk about personal PR, who are we talking about? We are talking about you and me. Personal PR is a subject which affects not only you but your client as well. It affects anyone with whom you come into contact. It is totally important to every area of life.

Good PR depends largely upon personality. Personality need not be static, nor is it something which has been wished upon us in childhood. Rather, personality can be developed—consciously as well as unconsciously.

As astrologers we can race ahead of the pack and come up a winner if we capture, store and release the energies available to us in an intelligent program of living.

We have easy access to the most complex index of individual energies and potentials that can be found. Once these are known and counseling techniques have been sharpened, we can shape and improve them with the object of building and bolstering personal PR. That index is the natal chart with its progressions which point out those times when action is needed to bring out our best qualities.

Even though the personality is expressed through the first horoscope house, it is necessary to read the entire chart. The persona of an individual is a complex bundle of personality—attitudes, abilities and personal characteristics.

Yet at times the natural expression of the personality does not totally reveal itself in the operation of its splendid qualities. This calls to mind two clients of mine who both have charts with Pisces on the Ascendant. They are both young men in their early thirties coming up the ranks of business. Their seeming serenity, sometimes apparent shyness and outer deportment often overshadows some of the other strong strains in their personalities and behavior.

It is not until you know and watch them put to the demanding test of coping with everyday problems that their wonderful qualities shine through what seems to be a lethargic approach to life. Knowing their horoscopes and working to stress the energies that enhance their personal PR has made a tremendous difference in the amount of success they are attracting as they advance up the executive ladder.

We, ourselves, can insure better PR with our clients, as well as with others who will aid in publicizing our services, by consulting our charts to improve our approach and demeanor. The thrust should target the improvement of communications, the lessening of apprehension, and avoiding tension.

Experts maintain that by being adaptable to new trends while at the same time holding conservatively to the proven methods of the past will bring success. In a way, this is mind boggling. Where does one draw the line? What is good and what is detrimental? Yet there is a great deal of sense tied to the notion when looked at in the light of that old adage: Change is the watch word of progression.

If you want to make a good impression on your client, refrain from meeting him at the door dressed like Cyndi Lauper, Boy George, or a variation of same, singing an operatic aria, or tap dancing to prove to him that you are an upbeat, positive person. Such aberrant behavior will only make him think you are a kook and is hardly guaranteed to win his respect.

A client is searching for someone calm and strong to help answer bothersome questions and/or solve his problems.

That brings to mind the manner of some so-called astrologers seen at the height of the public's interest in astrology in the 1960s. There was a lack of professional behavior which was prevalent across the country. It was not uncommon to spy an "astrologer" sitting on a straw mat in a yoga position out in the park giving a reading.

He claimed to be very spiritual because he took no fees in money. He did his work for the glory of mankind, a cheap bottle of wine, a snort or a joint. His attitude was anything but professional, he did hardly any counseling, if at all. Rather, he entertained and cajoled his "clients" with stories about their past lives and the karmic debts they were paying in this life. The "karma-cop-out" was very popular during that drop-out period.

Astrologer's Responsibility

Another attitude which needs to be examined is the astrologer's concept of his responsibility for the lives of his clients. He could feel as if he had their lives in his hands and that the client's welfare was wholly dependent upon the advice he gives them.

In some cases when a client returns for an update each year he discusses the same old problems again and again. In spite of receiving an intelligent, helpful delineation to work with, he does not seem to have made much progress at all. Some astrologers feel that it is their fault.

Untrue! No one can live another person's life. The astrologer is only responsible for giving the best counsel he can (not telling the client what to do) by offering a choice of suggested programs to help the client use his personal energies effectively.

Every professional is expected to give the best care and counsel that he can. This is an occupational must the same as that given in the prescription of a doctor, the car-care of a mechanic, or the counsel of a psychiatrist or psychologist. The dentist cannot force you to floss!

Importantly, the astrologer has an obligation to be sure that his counsel is suited to his client. To accomplish this he employs the client's chart as a guideline.

After acting in a morally responsible manner by encouraging the client to adopt certain changes in his life, an astrologer's work ends. Then it is up to the client to carry the ball and use his free will to make his own choices. Unless he does make those intellectual choices himself, his mental muscles will become flabby and useless.

Habit Systems

Counseling is a delicate operation, and your every action broadcasts a message to your client. Sometimes an appointment is made several weeks ahead of time. When that appointed day arrives you may be struck with the thought that you find it impossible to give a reading.

Unless you psych up your performance and keep the appointment, you are in danger of building up a self-defeating habit system leading to procrastination and a progressive lessening of performance.

In the beginning you were advised to give up any thoughts of a 40-hour week. So get into training. Build up your physical stamina. Then you will be better able to face the sometimes trying hours of the profession.

If you are overtaken by feelings of inadequacy, stop. Say a prayer to set the tone for the consultation. This will help you to cultivate a personal motivation that will bring confidence to your communication. In communicating with the client be sure to talk on his level.

Look as if you know what you are saying, even if there is a shadow of a doubt in your own mind. A flustering, nervous what'll-I-do-now attitude tends to cause the client to become uneasy and apprehensive.

Also, there is no shame in admitting that you do not know the answer to doubtful topics. Admit it. If you want to take the extra effort on behalf of your client, tell him you will research the matter and get back to him with the result.

If one of these doubtful moods overtakes you during the reading, excuse yourself. Step out of the office and compose yourself. Take a few deep breaths. Get the oxygen flowing to the brain. Tell yourself that you have a great opportunity here to help and serve and that you have been trained to do so. Return to the client and finish the consultation.

Sometimes the client's problems lead into strange and possibly shocking areas of life. If his concerns surprise, disgust, or even make you feel sick to your stomach, maintain a kindly, professional calm. Remember, an astrologer is a counselor, not a judge.

You are a professional if you are ready to address unusual and out-of-the-ordinary topics bothering your clientele. Can you keep your cool when they want help with sexual aberations or abuse, perverts, and/or deviates, business scams, other criminal acts, etc.? Prepare yourself.

Correct attitude and behavior are integral parts of the successful business pattern. In general, a counselor who encourages repeat business and the loyalty of his clients does not show-off to impress anyone and does not claim to know all of the universal secrets.

So that you may personally evaluate those areas which are prominent in your persona, the following test from the U. S. government can be used as a gauge.

RATING SCALE FOR EVALUATING PERSONAL TRAITS IMPORTANT TO THE PROPRIETOR OF A BUSINESS (Small Business Administration)

Evaluate yourself by placing a check mark by the trait that best describes you.

Initiative

Additional tasks sought; highly ingenious

Resourceful: alert to opportunities

Regular work performed without waiting for directions

Routine worker awaiting directions

Attitude Toward Others

Positive; friendly interest in people

Pleasant, polite

Sometimes difficult to work with

Inclined to be quarrelsome or uncooperative

Leadership

Forceful, inspiring confidence and loyalty

Order giver

Driver

Weak

Responsibility

Responsibility sought and welcomed

Accepted without protest

Unwilling to assume without protest

Avoided whenever possible

Organizing Ability

Highly capable of perceiving and arranging fundamentals in logical order

Able organizer

Fairly capable of organizing

Poor organizer

Industry

Industrious; capable of working hard for long hours

Can work hard, but not for too long a period

Fairly industrious

Hard work avoided

Decision

Quick and accurate

Good and careful

Quick, but often unsound

Hesitant & fearful

Sincerity

Courageous, squareshooter

On the level

Fairly sincere

Inclined to lack sincerity

Perseverance

Highly steadfast in purpose; not discouraged by obstacles

Effort steadily maintained

Average determination and persistence

Little or no persistence

Physical Energy

Highly energetic at all times

Energetic most of the time

Fairly energetic

Below average

8 WORK PROCEDURES

At first glance some of these procedures may seem "picky" and unnecessary. Be assured that using a businesslike approach starting with your first client will pay off handsomely later on when there are so many demands upon your time. The system and order you establish at the beginning eventually become habits and that follow through will prove to be the biggest prevention against wasting time.

According to time management specialist Patrick J. Montana, president of the National Center for Career Life Planning, "We spend 80% of our time on unimportant things that produce only 20% of the results."

The same idea is also held by others, such as waste managers or efficiency experts. Your payoff will result from reading about these categories, then applying what you have learned to your work habits. Not only will you be able to handle your workload easier, you will be surprised at how much less time it will consume to accomplish that work. Time is not only money, it allows for the expansion of pertinent knowledge and invites better health due to less tension permeating the environment.

The message of these experts is plain to see. How long does it take to do so and so? Does the fee we charge cover that time in addition to the fixed expenses associated with the procedure?

Entrepreneurs claim that a growing, successful business can be improved from time to time by clocking work procedures. This yard stick is probably more significant in a small business. Become your own recovery of time engineer.

Whether a business is large or small, studies show that almost everyone wastes two hours or more a day. If you work a five day week, that means that ten hours would be spent doing nonessentials. This same percentage of productivity was also found in the habits of students and housewives.

These findings indicate that we need to do a bit of self analysis to redirect our energies into more productive work habits. Then it will be easier for us to meet deadlines without becoming impatient and frustrated.

Environmental Impact

When you attend the theatre, you expect to sit back and be entertained. When you go to a dance hall, you expect to be active and socialize. When you go to church you expect to be reverent and attentive. These places provide a certain environment where set patterns of behavior are exhibited naturally and automatically.

Does this happen when you enter your own work space? What kind of program does the place broadcast? If you have spent a good deal of your time there playing cards, reading gossip magazines or romance novels, or even entertaining friends with parties, the pull to get down to business at hand is absent.

By analyzing and contrasting these surroundings, you can sense immediately how habit systems are influenced by environment. An important addition to your office, then, is a vibration that inspires productivity. When you step into the atmosphere, you should feel like plunging into your work without a thought of procrastination. There is nothing comparable to the psychological lift of viewing a job well done.

Priority of Tasks

Because astrologers usually work alone, it is exceptionally easy for them to waste time. We need to learn how to get things done promptly and efficiently while at the same time taking every opportunity to plant growth seeds. Whether in your office, social life, or at home, this habit system should become an unconscious on-going process.

It is human nature to tackle the easiest and most familiar tasks first and let the more important or difficult one take second place. The hard chores, or those jobs that force you to meet deadlines fall into the same classification. So the first step in establishing a solid program of time management is to set up a system of the proper priorities which separate those things we do to earn a living from the leisure activities that give us pleasure.

Taking an inventory of how you spend your time on the job will probably produce some surprising results. You will find that a lot of your time and energy has been frittered away with little accomplishment to show for it. Another way to waste time is to flit from task to task like a butterfly; never finishing one job before going on to another.

Remember the Bible's admonition: "Consider the lilies of the field, how they grow, they toil not, neither do they spin." Matthew 6:28. Be sure you are both a toiler and a spinner to be a success at anything in life.

Many successful business people learn to work anywhere. I have heard some would-be astrologers claim they could not start their practice because they did not have a filing cabinet. This is a cop-out. At first, any cardboard box can handle your files.

To be effective, you do not need a plethora of highly expensive equipment. All you need to start is the desire, the education, and the intellect. The accoutrements can always be added later.

Procrastination is so easy to follow, especially under certain astrological aspects. Sometimes the subconscious mind jumps onto any excuse to use as a wedge against us getting on with our plans.

As the impressionable Moon stands for that subconscious mind, we can understand the over-adaptability that might stimulate actions to turn to easier things rather than toeing the line, so to speak.

That mood can be put down pronto if we consciously set aside anything which would interfere with our demonstration of personal plans. Like other successful people we should learn to work anywhere—on a plane, in a line at the bank or checkout counter, waiting in a dentist or doctor office, as well as in whatever space we use for an office.

Mode of Operation

Another custom that works extremely well for the successful business person is to make a list of things you would like to accomplish or steps on those "in the works" projects at night before you quit for the day.

When your next day starts you will know just exactly what you want to do. This saves a lot of time shuffling papers; accepting and then rejecting one idea of work after another until a decision is made as just where to begin until there is no time left to do anything! True, there will always be interuptions and you probably will never be able to go straight down the list to tick off these chores. But having a step-by-step program will take you closer to your goal of accomplishment than a hit or miss method ever could.

By concentrating on doing one thing at a time, all of your mental power is directed to the project. Your vital energies for creativity needed to complete the job are directed in such an organized pattern that you have speeded up the whole course of action.

A priceless way to use mental strength developed this way is to direct it into a project that has been "bugging" you. You know the kind; we have all suffered through them. You mull it over and can hardly decide how to handle the factors involved. Where should you begin? How should you handle the meat of the thing? Then—how much or how little information should be included? After these decisions are made and action taken, you are free to proceed to another task.

When you complete one of these "hard" chores, a certain feeling of accomplishment infuses you. It develops and sustains your self-confidence. As a result, other tasks seem easy by comparison. That marvelous buoyancy carries you on to the next item on your list of chores.

A noticeable manifestation in the mind of an active person is how the subconscious has a tendency to solve job problems while the objective brain is otherwise occupied. Especially does this action take place when we are at leisure or involved in recreational pursuits, such as playing golf, tennis, watching television, reading a book and the like.

Ideas come through as if out of the blue. They nudge their way up onto the screen of your mind in a flash. Because we are usually otherwise occupied, the idea does not stay there long. We need to catch it at the moment of its objective formation—our first consciousness of it.

One of the best ways to capture these thoughts is to keep a pencil and pad in several places at home, near the bed, the television set or where you sit most often; also it is a good idea to keep pencil and pad in your purse or briefcase. Don't forget your car! A pad, or better yet, a cassette tape recorder will serve. You should not take a chance on forgetting one of those splendid ideas after they hatch all of a sudden in your objective brain only to fade as fast as they appeared.

Selective Decision Making

Another contributing factor towards success is learning to make decisions about trifles speedily. Learn to separate the essentials from the nonessentials. Recognize that many of the decisions we are called upon to make are minor ones. To consume an exorbitant amount of time to solve minor problems is a poor work habit.

Decide immediately these minor questions and let the chips fall where they may. Of course, your major decisions should be allotted as much time as needed. Sometimes these may even call for a consultation with another professional, such as your accountant, your lawyer, your printer, or a colleague astrologer.

Everyone recognizes that lost messages, missed phone calls, files that cannot be found, forms, letterheads and other supplies that have run out erect barriers to getting work completed on time. The answer is to anticipate the needs associated with running the everyday routine of your practice.

After your business has expanded, you will find that an answering service or machine and a computer will be indispensible in keeping the work flow going smoothly. Your tape recorder will serve many purposes. Be sure it has a silent pause switch. Also, if there is an on/off switch in the hand mike, this will free the other hand to turn pages in reference books or charts when doing tapes to be mailed.

For one reason or another you will probably use your tape recorder a great deal more than you first thought you would. This will use up a lot of batteries. Buy the best batteries by the carton, seal them in plastic, and store them in your refrigerator for longlife operation.

This is an area where it definitely does not pay to be penny wise and pound foolish! Your time is your most valuable commodity. Having a battery fail in the midst of your consultation can be excessively expensive in time lost—to say nothing of the broken train of thoughts.

Flexible Organization

System and organization form the backbone of an efficient business. With an astrological practice, every client should be handled in the same manner, despite the few orders which are complicated. Regardless of the service ordered—whether it is for a mail or personal consultation—set up guidelines of how to handle each work function.

Before you open the door for business during the gestation period, you should invest plenty of time thinking about these procedures. With this mental (or better physically written) list once decided upon, each time a service is enacted there will be no need to rethink the process. You will merely have to refer to the work outline. Then as you expand, you will no doubt revamp these approaches to embrace all of your services. In that way you will be able to keep current the guidelines for conducting your practice most effectively.

At the office:

1. Solicit business by providing a flyer describing your services. See chapter 12 for more information.

2. Do not start work until the fee (or retainer fee) and the signed release form with the complete birth data is in hand. Check carefully to see if all pertinent data is available so that you can start the work.

3. Prepare the work. Some astrologers ask for a questionnaire to be filled in (extent of questions varies with different practitioners), or some counselors schedule a preconsultation session to get the information needed.

4. Do all the work to prepare for the reading. Assess natal chart, progressions, transits with case history in relation to client's needs.

5. Personal consultation with client. Astrologer records the session and gives the tape to the client. Psychologists claim that people retain only about ten percent of what they hear only once. If the client has the tape he can listen to it many times. He should be encouraged to listen for inspiration at times of his low mood swings. (That demands positive wording on the astrologer's part.) Also, if the client had a tape of the session, he cannot claim that the astrologer said something he did not—things of an unprofessional nature or hard predictions.

Some astrologers also keep copies of the tapes, but that can become unwieldly in a short time if you have many clients and do not own a warehouse.

Through the mail:

1. Solicit business. Send forms and information.

2. After receiving fee, signed release and questionnaire, make sure all the basic facts are recorded.

3. Tape the reading. Don't put it off too long. Remember that the post office has a regulation that a client must receive his mail order within thirty days. After that he can sue.

Packaging Your Product

You probably realize that the packaging of your presentation will determine your success to a large extent—especially if you mail it. This will affect your repeat business. In the first mailing, send your tapes acompanied by a neatly drawn horoscope in a padded mailing envelope. To make the postage work for you, insert flyers about your other services, products, activities, or books for sale.

An astrological reading can be included in the group of specialty items and should be handled accordingly. So send it "certified mail—return receipt requested" to get a receipt returned announcing when it was delivered and who accepted it. Your fee should cover all of these incidentals (tapes, postage, special handling, forms or whatever). Successful business people say a product should be handled and shaped to the requirements of the customer.

Excitation Follow-up

Customer handling does not end there. As in other businesses a common practice is called stimulation or excitation, which includes acts taken to encourage the client to engage you for return business.

Don't let your clients think you have a bad memory, or that you take their fee and forget them. Keep a tickler list of when to contact them again.

Then on the listed tickler date, phone or write the client a few weeks before an interesting transit triggers his active chart. Discuss the interpretation of that configuration briefly and suggest he make an appointment for an update reading.

Your tickler list could also include dates on which to send birthday cards and/or Christmas cards as a reminder to your regular clients.

Keep Learning

Being ready and anxious to help others through your craft, you should realize that you can do so only to the extent of your training, ability and experience. Broaden your knowledge as much as possible and be aware of better counseling techniques. Learn something from each consultation. These approaches will expand your usefulness and attract more success.

9 BURNOUT AND THE BLAHS

From a study based on interviews with 884 workers, a sociologist at the University of Minnesota says job overload is the major cause of stress and burnout.

Work overload to an astrologer usually stems from his promising a number of clients to complete certain services within a set amount of time. He begins to feel pushed as the deadlines near. Stress starts to build. Before long the responsibility of meeting these deadlines builds up pressure. Then he experiences either the blahs or burnout.

Age has a lot to do with how much it takes before burnout sets in. The sociological study mentioned above was conducted in six groups of men and women. It revealed that people stabilize in work environments with age. These older workers are less likely to be called upon to adapt to new work situations.

As far as astrologers go, perhaps chronological age would not play as important a part as the number of years they had been counseling.

Even an old pro can look at the symbol for Neptune in a horoscope and draw a mental blank as far as interpreting it is concerned. At such times there is nothing stimulated through association in the subconscious mind. At those times we have to prime the pump. Then is when keywords come in handy.

Stop straining and doodle. Draw Neptune. Now scribble words associated with Neptune on the paper. Then check its aspects and the houses its energy flows through. Assign positive words for the supportive aspects and precautionary words for the restrictive aspects.

After such an exercise, your gray cells of the brain should be stimulated enough to bring to your objective consciousness the communication which flows into an intelligent reading.

A helpful reference book aiding in this ritual of priming the mental pump is Lynne Palmer's *ABC Basic Chart Reading*[1]. Therein you will see both supportive and restrictive connotations for all of the chart elements, including planets, houses and aspects. If the burnout is not serious, this application of keywords will aid in squelching the problem.

At the opposite swing of your work pendulum you may at times discover another phenomena. How about those periods when you feel sluggish because there is a low demand for your services? You experience a feeling of loss and haven't the slightest idea of what to do about it. Do you become apprehensive and ready to give up the whole venture at such times?

You can lick that source of frustration by branching out in the astrology field. Write articles or books; conduct classes, lectures, workshops or seminars; take a computer course at a local college in order to accomplish more with your training.

There will be a two-fold reward for engaging in such activities. Not only will these projects broaden your knowledge, they will allow you to publicize your work and show how you can serve your community. A sense of satisfaction and self-confidence will replace the burnout.

Another condition, not as drastic as burnout, that can gnaw away at your valuable time and even prevent you from making deadlines, is a temporary lagging of interest. Sometimes termed the 4 p.m. blahs, this attitude may rob you of an hour or more each day. That adds up to a considerable total of lost and wasted time, eventually money as well.

Sometimes these blahs strike earlier in the day—even at 2 p.m., when a person has had too much to eat or drink at noon.

An observant person can spot the blahs immediately. He notices that the worker with the blahs unconsciously begins to sharpen pencils,

---

[1]AFA, Tempe, AZ

shuffle papers, go to the restroom, get a drink of water, doodle on scrap pads, write useless memos and the like.

Psychotherapist Barbara Mackoff, author of *Leaving the Office Behind,* claims that to prevent this lag of interest we should lower our expectations of what can be accomplished at the end of the day.

The solution to these blah moods appears to be an individual matter. For the fun of it, I asked twelve people what they did when they got burnout or experienced the blahs. Their answers:

1. Take a long walk in the park
2. Go for a ride along the ocean
3. Get a job transfer
4. Change directions by entering politics
5. Go into meditation
6. Quit the job
7. Go to night school for diversion
8. Watch television
9. Read part of a novel
10. Change concentration by working on another task
11. Nap for ten minutes
12. Talk to someone about unrelated topics

Perhaps the variety of comments stems from the fact that these people were different ages, worked at different jobs. Some were in managerial positions and others, not.

However, their answers all reveal one fact: The mind demands a shifting of gears before it can pick up and carry on again. Doing something unreleated to the work for a short time helps to solve the problem of boredom, burnout and the blahs.

10 PUBLICITY AND MARKETING

It pays to take particular care and spend considerable time when deciding how you will be able to reach your customers. There are many avenues for this activity open to you. However, some will pay off better in one community than in another. Sometime a little trial and error may be necessary and wise before making a final decision.

To build up a business and keep it growing and increasing you need to let your public know what you have to offer. The name of the game is publicity.

Astrologers have all run into a certain negative attitude toward astrology by the public at large. Even though the subject is centuries old, as yet it has not reached the point of reverent respect given other present-day, service-oriented professions.

Astrologers have been and still are their own worst enemies. Many of them dislike being told that they must conform to the norm. But let's face it. The 60s are over! The hippie era is past! You cannot appear in front of an audience as did one astrologer in sandals and dirty toenails and expect to be respected by the general public. They get turned off by preternatural physical appearance and behavior.

By the same token, you must speak intelligently to the things that clients want to hear about. They do not want to be told in great detail about their karma; and they do not want to be told about fatalistic things. They come for reassurance, answers and inspiration. A well trained astrologer can give them those things along with the chart interpretation.

This does not mean lying to your client. What it does mean is the proper application of astrology to bring out and emphasize the positive indications in the horoscope and showing how the client has a choice in counteracting the negative, restrictive influences by a positive attitude and the redirection of available energy.

In this approach there is no such thing as a bad planet, house, sign or aspect in the chart. These are merely symbols of energy. The counselor who knows his astrology understands proper counseling techniques and can always come up with a helpful suggestion that, even though it may not eliminate the client's problem, it will provide him a route to follow out of his quandry.

Once an astrologer gets a negative reputation, it is extremely difficult to overcome. It may take years; it may never be done. Think of the pretty high school girl who has "gone all the way with a boy" only to discover within a week that she has the reputation of being the town whore. Just as a young girl must guard her reputation, so should every astrologer, because a bad reputation is practically impossible to overcome in this field.

So if you send your client off with a satisfied and more confident feeling, he will discuss his satisfaction with others. This is the best way to insure business growth and to let people know about your good reputation.

Another thing! Appearing at psychic fairs and reading cards, palms or tea leaves and doing other things that some people advertise does not make the reader a professional in this field. As soon as we take the word astrology and qualify it by saying, "Oh, I also read chicken entrails, I throw dice, do sand readings, spread cards!", you lose your legitimacy as a professional. A true professional astrologer bases his work on astrology.

When you think over the foregoing comments, it is easy to understand that publicizing your services properly takes in a wide territory and is perhaps the most difficult task for an astrology counselor to do.

The Yellow Pages

First, let us consider the Yellow Pages published by the telephone company, the Chamber of Commerce, or a local businessman's organization. Because the phone may be the first contact that a client has with you, how you advertise in the phone books as well as how you answer the phone and describe your services either can help or hinder in building up your personal public image.

The impressions reflected by your advertisement in the phone book and how you handle the calls (whether live or recorded) can also play a strong role in educating the public about astrology and just what it is that an ethical astrologer does. Technique and manners are directly related in selling yourself and your product.

In most areas of the country now, Yellow Pages have sections for astrologers, astrology, and/or astrology schools. This is the area in which your ad will appear. You will notice that under this general heading are listed other mystical, occult or metaphysical ads. There is nothing you can do about that. However, you do have control about what goes into your space so that you will not be classed in with Madame Mabella.

The ad should appear dignified and professional. Make sure that spiritualistic, mediumistic or occult references are not included. An astrologer is not a fortune teller in the predictive sense of the word. He should be especially careful not to give the impression that he is, even though it is not uncommon for an astrolger to develop his psychic senses.

Reaching the widest number of people demands a middle-of-the-road technique—neither too hep nor too staid. Later when you know more about your client, you can swing either way to reach his level. When in doubt, use basic English. After all, counseling from his chart demands a free flow of communication.

It is not uncommon for an astrolger to receive phone calls at any hour of the day or night. This does not mean he is ethically bound to answer—especially at three o'clock in the morning. Of course, this problem does not occur if your business is not in your home.

In either case, an office phone or a home phone should be attached to an answering machine (if you do not engage an answering service—a business expense). A recorded message may prevent the loss of business. You would be able to hear comments from both old and new clients. Remember that a satisfied customer is your best advertising.

You need to put some thought into the message on your answering machine. It should embrace items something like this "This is Doris Chase Doane. I am not by the phone right now. Please leave your name and phone number including the area code at the sound of the tone. Thank you for calling." Or, you might add the information as to when you are available by phone, such as "between 10 a.m. and 4 p.m."

Promotional Activities

To aid in establishing and/or increasing your business, branch out into other activities where you can contact a wider public and become better known as an astrological counselor.

Some people learn to write or lecture, both attention-getting devices. Find out what talent you have in either or both pursuits. After all, nothing ventured, nothing gained! Start by writing for local astrology newsletters or magazines. At first you may not get paid, but this is a way to pay your dues, so to speak.

Your reward will come through advertising your expertise and allowing your name to be associated with astrology. This may lead to supplemental income from writing articles or books—income from which could help support your business.

Lecture at community groups, chamber of commerce, men's clubs, women's clubs, high schools, colleges, luncheon meetings and elsewhere. The program chairmen of all such organizations are crying for lecturers and provide an excellent jumping off place for beginners.

Another avenue which offers opportunities to publicize your image and services is to teach astrology classes at local colleges, the YMCA, or other places where people gather. Also, to get into the local swing of things, join the Chamber of Commerce and/or the Better Business Bureau in your community. Splendid contacts can be made there.

Your business cards can be handed out at these activities, placed on bulletin boards, such as at schools, markets, the laundromat and areas where people gather or pass through. Always carry a supply of your business cards with you, because you can never anticipate all of the opportunities to pass them out.

When you become active in social groups and club affairs, tell your friends and neighbors about your business. Ask them to pass the word along to other people—especially that you are available for counseling.

Another way to advertise your service is through the party plan. Either you or a friend of yours throws a party, and you are featured as the astrologer. You can give a general talk about astrology and this can be followed by brief references to each sign of the zodiac, giving the birthdates within which the sign is included. This may even be conducted as a charity for a church, the Scouts, a boys club or the like. Then the small donations collected at the door can be given to your friend for her pet charity.

Local public television stations usually hold an auction of varied donated goods and services once a year to gain funds to help run the station. These drives present another opportunity to gain publicity. Offer a reading or two by sending in a nicely designed and printed certificate showing your name, address and phone number and the type of reading, with its paid-in-advance fee.

Another idea: Contact a shop that specializes in birthday and gift goods. Arrange to have literature describing you and your services on display. Include an application for a reading. Then promise the gift shop owner a certain percentage of all readings that are ordered.

Business Image

In addition to the above ways to publicize your services, the idea of personal packaging, your image, should be taken with extreme seriousness. There is no question about it, many professionals want to be judged by their talents, but instead they are often judged upon their appearance. The old adage holds: First impressions count.

Image is not vain, phony or foolish. It should be considered as a business skill—a tool we can use to expand toward success. To reiterate this idea is an incident experienced by Barbara Blaes, image consultant, when she explains how audiences react to the way we dress.

At professional meetings, she gradually became aware that the men looked like professionals, while most of the women looked like support staff, even though they were giving reports and held highly responsible positions.

Ms. Blaes said: "At one particular meeting a woman got up to give a report. She was dressed in a pink polyester pant suit. She was at least half way through her talk before I realized that she really had something to say. I was stunned! I had discounted her because she did not *look* to me like an authority."

If you do not think that such a reaction is truly important, please read the book entitled *Twice Over Lightly,*[1] by two famous and respected women: actress Helen Hayes and author Anita Loos. On pages 101-105 they tell about their meeting with Lynne Palmer, PMAFA, at her astrology school in New York City.

They had made their appointment and gone fully expecting to meet some gypsy-like person in batik and amber beads with a bandeau around her forehead and wearing a full multicolored skirt, only to be confronted by an intelligent, sophisticated woman in a Chanel suit. Their surprise is carefully documented and their admiration of astrologers (at least of the Lynne Palmer variety) in unbounded.

If we want astrology to be generally accepted by the public at large as an honorable profession, we must all make the same positive impression on those with whom we come into contact.

Too many professional astrologers are self-defeating, by their attitude, environment and/or dress. Advertising yourself as a card reader, psychic, medium, or anything but a pure astrologer demeans our profession.

That is not to say that other occult regimes and approaches to life's problems are inaccurate. Merely, that we have our hands full correcting the public's definition of what an astrologer is and does.

Dressing like an unmade bed makes an equally negative impression. To be grouped with professionals, like it or not, we must dress and

---

[1]Harcourt Brace Jovanovich, NYC, 1972

act like professional people in public. That means to conform to the general norm.

In my professional capacity, I have heard thousands of complaints, including one woman who said after seeing an astrologer, "It took hours to remove the cat hairs from my clothes!" What she said about the consultation does not bear repeating in polite company. I gave her another reading to save face for my colleagues. I also told her that she should check on the reader's certification before firming any appointments.

Newspapers

Personally, I have never found newspaper ads in large city newspapers to be effective in drumming up business. In smaller places, the newspaper should be used only if a local hook can be placed in the ad or its accompanying writeup.

Newspaper reporters rely on the public for their stories. So you should stimulate your creativity to think of ways to give them information that they will want to print. If you appear before a social club you can publicize your activities and credits in the society pages.

In the case of newspapers with larger circulations, you might be called upon to pay for an ad in order to have your story published as a news item. In either case learn to write a publicity release, whether you are interviewed by a reporter or not. Also, have a resume of your accomplishments and credits in the astrology field, such as the various certificates you have gained or the awards and citations you have. Include conferences in which you have appeared, schools at which you have taught, official positions in astrology groups you have held and the like.

Still another avenue for exposure is the Letters to the Editor column. Utilize this readers' forum to pass along ideas that will further your image or your work in the community.

Publicity Release

Experience is a valued commodity. If possible, get some practice in writing publicity releases even if the job does not pay up-front cash.

Such was my background which came from activities without fees when I first jumped into the game. I became publicity chairman for two organizations at once—the Alliance of Fine Arts and the United Amateur Press Association. For several years, it was my duty to send out press releases to the media—print, radio and in its infancy television.

This type of training was excellent in teaching me the numerous ways an appropriate release can be utilized and placed in the proper medium to educate the public to certain facts. There are three areas of significance in a press release.

1. The release must be typed double spaced on 8½ x 11 white paper with wide margins to allow for editorial remarks.

2. In the upper right hand corner, type your name, address and phone number so that the media can get back to you if necessary. Then in the lefthand top corner type in the release date.

3. In the first paragraph make brief references to *who, what, where, when and how* of the event so that the *essential* information is included. That first paragraph may be all that is published or aired. So it is vitally important! Follow with other short paragraphs (most important first) such as describing the lecture topic, biography of speaker, or other pertinent data.

Such a publicity release, along with a personal resume and a clear, black and white, glossy photo of yourself, can be sent to the program director or host of a local talk show. If you are engaged to appear, use your own initiative to publicize the fact. Plan to hold a press party by all means either before or after the interview.

Branching Out

If you anticipate opening an astrology bookstore or starting an astrology school to supplement your income as well as educate the public, be sure to think about and use appropriately all of these publicity angles. Before taking action, choose an electional chart during the time your own chart shows support for these enterprises. At that time of the chart have a grand opening party. Be sure to invite the press to the party. Have your press release and resumé along with a program of activities available to be passed around.

Thinking of picking a time to open up reminds me of one of my clients, who asked me to do just that for a metaphysical book store she planned to establish and operate. When I checked the ephemeris for the positions of the planets, I found that all that year there were unfavorable aspects formed between the slow moving planets. You guessed it! As a result the trials charts looked anything but promising. I advised her to wait and not take action at the time.

But she did not want to wait! Her enthusiasm was bubbling at the idea of getting started. She could not be persuaded to hold off and asked me to select a chart with the best support possible even though these long-time aspects were within operative orb of aspecting each other.

I tackled the job, which proved to be one of the most difficult selections of a chart I have ever run across. The only way I know to solve such a dilemma is to place the planets that are mapped in heavy affliction in the least important houses to the business.

The hour I finally came up with was an ungodly time—after one o'clock in the morning. I suggested that she invite her friends and neighbors to a champagne party and arrange with one of them to be sure to purchase a book at the minute of the electional chart. This would vitalize the project.

Her soirée was well attended; everyone had a great time. She totaled a most satisfactory income from the book sales on that one night alone. She was thrilled and figured the business was well on the way to huge success, but her buoyant enthusiasm became her downfall. Right after that auspicious and prosperous opening night, she promptly ordered ten copies of every book listed in several wholesale catalogues, many of which sold slowly.

It goes without saying that her business was a failure; not because of the charted time, but due to her lack of experience. Anyone in the occult book business knows that certain titles sell hardly any copies at all. Usually they are reference books needed by a very few, or books about subjects of little interest to many book buyers.

Her ignorance in knowing how to stock such a store overrode the splendid publicity she had, the overwhelming response on opening night and the initial support of friends. Sustaining that enormous inventory did her business into bankruptcy.

In either of the enterprises involving teaching or bookselling, certain practical experience is essential. A super way to come by this know-how is to become an apprentice or "gofer" to one already in the business. Then when you, yourself, are the boss in your own business, you will know what your employees should do to educate the customers or students as well as the general public.

In a book store, you should give your clerks lessons so that they can answer questions, recommend astrology books, study materials and other astrology related items. In running a school, you must design a program and show your teachers how to follow the basic outlines in a graduated curriculum.

Why Publicity?

That is the title of an article in the March 21, 1985 AFA *Bulletin* by Lynne Palmer. Here is an excerpt:

"Do you realize that publicity entails more than merely appearing on a show or doing a newspaper interview? It means getting your name known . . . About five years ago, a press agent quoted me his prices. I was shocked to learn that his fee was $21,000 for a ten-city tour for radio, TV and press coverage, and I would have to pay all expenses as well, including air fare, hotel and food! Now this was *not* a famous press agent at all—they would charge $50,000 a year with several years running contract."

She adds, "To hire a press agent is costly and no one knows better than you how to promote yourself." And in the last analysis, it is really up to each of us to do the job.

Palmer's book *Do-It-Yourself Publicity Directory*[1] contains information rarely found in one package. An indispensible reference, it provides all of us with invaluable ideas about enhancing our image and drumming up business.

---

[1]American Federation of Astrologers, Tempe, AZ

11 COUNSELING

How you handle your clients will determine in large part if you can build up a sense of credibility and respect.

Just as every situation is different, every client is an individual. Therefore, any automatic, systematic 1-2-3 approach planned to be used with each and every client would hardly address their needs and special desires.

Any of the many different areas in their lives could be the basis of their particular problems. The most common concerns involve money, love and job complications. The background fabric of a client's thoughts, feelings and actions reflects his motivation and conditioning. The best method of obtaining this type of data is with the aid of a personal case history. See Chapter 12 for an example.

A case history benefits both the astrolger and the client. The astrologer can better handle the client's needs. The client comes into a better realization of his background and usually then can see the sense of the counseling program suggested to him more readily. He should realize how associating your recommendations with his needs will help him to cultivate more control over his personal affairs.

You may think that a case history is too time consuming and a waste of your valuable time to bother with. But even a short history will assist you in your work and influence the client to build up a respect and credibility for you as a professional.

A professional person is expected to operate much as a physician or an attorney does. Before any kind of diagnosis is made, a doctor must have a patient's case history. Then he is able to prescribe for the patient's benefit a helpful therapy. Likewise, a lawyer expects the cooperation of his client when he assembles the facts of a situation. Then he is able to suggest an approach which will handle the client's problem.

Redirecting Energies

Learn to fashion a program for your client that will bring more satisfaction and happiness into his life style. Aside from the basic natal chart and its progressions and transits, do not overlook the unlimited scope and effectiveness in measuring chart energies with the cosmodyne method.

This application of cosmodynes is amply described and demonstrated on actual horoscopes in my books *Vocational Selection and Counseling,* Volume I and II, published by the AFA. Volume I discusses counseling techniques, and Volume II actually demonstrates them.

To counsel competently there is a strong need to expand practical astrology into an astro-therapeutic tool that directs itself to the physical, emotional and mental body—and addresses restrictive energies as well as the counseling of harmonious energy.

In other words, the client's needs and desires concern factors relating to various planes of experience. Thus horoscope interpretation naturally falls into three areas or levels: (1) The physical, personal, material level; (2) the feeling and mental level; (3) the esoteric, spiritual level.

To put their problems into focus, we may need to draw from all three levels. At other times, treating a client's problem may be handled by probing only one or two areas. As the able astrologer assembles the client's deep-seated concerns, he can prepare himself ahead of time to choose the separate levels of the persona involved. This will insure that the client's search for specific helpful guidance will be explored thoroughly.

An astrologer should never limit himself. Through study, practice and experience you will be able to develop a knowledge of counseling that can be used in the myriad of situations confronting you. After all, astrology provides viable and valuable treatment techniques through the language of symbolism. These treatments can be applied to the complex physiological and sociological stress we see on every hand.

Even though sometimes a client may not seem deeply disturbed on the surface, we should ever realize that in the remotest corner of his mind may lurk dark mental images of the nature symbolized by the restricted planets in his horoscope.

As astrologers we should be aware of one or all of these areas in order to get to the heart of the client's conflict. By assessing this wide spectrum of activity, we are better able to encourage him to develop coping strategies that will assist in replacing unwanted situations with more positive actions, thus allowing him to gain and maintain self control.

Objectivity

An active professional astrologer, like a doctor, counsels for the problem, keeping an open mind. If you have studied and applied your craft and know how to follow the rules, it will hardly be necessary for you to compare your chart with that of a would-be client in order to make a decision as to whether you should accept that client or not.

Your objectivity should also expand to the point where you are confident in the understanding of where your responsibility ends. Even if your client does not fulfill his greatest potential (as few do), you should hold a strong thought that you have done your best to guide him in his proper direction. You are not God anymore than a psychiatrist is. You both are professionals who may have patients unfortunately unsuccessful in overcoming their difficulties through no fault of their counselor.

Remember the old adage: "You can lead a horse to water; you can't make him drink!" The finest astrologer can give the best advice in the world only to see the client blithely ignore it.

Another area into which your objectivity should be focussed is the ending of a reading—that is, in the one-to-one type where the client comes to your office in person. As you know all too well, a doctor does not let his patient talk to him for two hours or so after the diagnosis and prescribed treatment has been discussed. Your counseling falls into the same service-oriented pattern. You should follow the doctor's example. Remember, time is money.

Learn how to use kindness and patience, yet firmness, in preventing a client from lingering.

Highlights

In public libraries you will find many books on counseling. Reading them will give you helpful ideas about how to conduct your work. Even though such books are directed to their fields of counseling, they present basic fundamentals common to all areas of counseling. These approaches should interest you as you may be able to apply them to your performance.

But you may be even more interested in some highlights gleaned from a rap session of professional astrologers. The theme of the group discussion was "counseling and handling clients." The following list recorded at that session should provide you with good food for thought.

—Keep direct eye contact with your client.

—Keep lines of communication open. Don't cross your arms or legs, and avoid postures that give the impression of aloofness.

—Remain relaxed to put your client at ease. Sometimes his apprehensive state or unreasoning fear of the future can overpower his logical thought processes.

—Your responsibility is to bring out the positive confidence so that your client can solve his own problems. That thought should be nourished. There is good in all of us (sometimes obvious—sometimes not), but it is there to be cultivated.

—Express your thoughts on a kind and impersonal level. Try not to let your client sidestep important issues.

—Deal with actual thoughts and emotions. Gently prevent a client from avoiding discussion of his behavior.

—Encourage clients to face up to and admit repressions, poor self-attitudes and other negative traits.

—When a client starts to explore an area of help, or the counselor wishes to recommend outside assistance, such as a lawyer, doctor, clinic, or whatever, consult the list of such professionals and hotlines referred to in Chapter 12.

—Insecure clients need approval and constant assurance while they are learning to become self-confident.

—Use concrete, basic language and address the problem rather than skirting it with vague inuendoes.

—Avoid the use of red ink in front of a client. This point started a heated discussion at the session. This was questioned by several astrologers who always placed the progressed positions in red ink around the natal chart. The answer came that due to a few clients' vulnerability they thought the red ink stood for bad signs in their horoscopes. There was no agreement on this point.

—Be careful not to predict death or any other dramatic failure.

—Avoid anything which might shock, dazzle, stun, disturb or upset the client emotionally.

—Be sure to approach the client's problems from a positive angle (never use negative words) by stressing his natural attributes.

—Tape the session. Then he can play the tape should he feel depressed. The upbeat, positive flow will help him to lift himself out of a down-beat mood. Not only that, it will remind him of the things he should stress so as to turn his life around toward happiness and success.

12 THE LAST WORD

Before closing our discussion of astrology as a business, there are several odds and ends to bring to your attention. These various items should provide enough mental stimulation to stir your creativity into action so that you can attract more success to your venture.

The more you know about the world in all of its aspects, and how you put that knowledge to use for your client, is the solid base that insures a strong, healthy growth for your business. Your client functions in the world's business, political and social environment. Keeping up-to-date in these areas allows access to splendid current material which will help you to counsel with greater success.

To accomplish getting this know-how, read current journals, bulletins, and magazines, such as *Newsweek, Time, U. S. News and World Report,* the *Wall Street Journal,* and others that present information of all kinds: finances, health, hobbies, travel, jobs, etc. It goes without saying that you should keep abreast of current astrological literature to be found in the *AFA Bulletin,* the *Astrological Journal,* and others.

Many of these publications, as well as books on the subjects or fees for clipping services on specific subjects, may be tax deductible. In any case, more success can be attracted through the useful and appropriate application of a wide knowledge from all fields. This was discussed in Chapter 2.

Your Reference Library

Every professional doctor, lawyer, accountant, as well as astrologer should own an adequate reference library. He will need one not only to counsel clients successfully but to maintain a high professional level using correct grammar and proper English to present material to the public in a skilled, expert form.

Your general library should contain dictionaries, synonym books, atlases, encyclopedias and the like. Old geography books found in second hand book stores help in finding places that have gone off the map or were too small to put on the map in the first place. To start your own astrological library I would suggest that you write and ask for the reference reading directory composed by the Educational Committee of the American Federation of Astrologers.

If you use a computer, or are thinking of purchasing one, the most complete list of computers, software, etc. is to be found in the AFA Product Price List, published by the same organization. They also have experts available who will answer questions relating to the whole area of computers and software.

Birth Certificates

When you go to the Department of Vital Statistics in the town or city of birth, be fully prepared. Give the clerk the proper information which should include the birth month, day and year, as well as the names of both parents. Ask for the birth certificate (not the birth registration).

In some offices all of the data is recorded on microfilm. Others use record albums, filing cards or computers. In any case, most times the clerk will search for the information. However, in a few instances, the clerk may allow you to look for it yourself, especially if you are known to him as a researcher of a non-profit organization. Procedures vary from office to office, and from clerk to clerk.

If you are unable to go to the office in person, contact your State Vital Statistics Department (usually located in the capitol city of the state). There you will find a record book called *The Source*. In its "Appendix F" is listed the proper department or bureau to contact in each state, as well as the dates for which certificates are recorded.

Also, see "Recording of Vital Statistics" on page 192 in my book *Time Changes in USA.*[1] Address to contact in each state is given.

The charge for a copy of a birth certificate is usually $3 to $5, but fees change constantly. For a quick accurate response, send for one record at a time and do not write any unnecessary words to distract the clerk. The only extra mention might be a request for the recorded hour of birth. Don't say why you want it; the clerk could care less.

Many states offer copies of birth certificates only to the native; no one else. That is because people were picking up phony certificates in order to get passports, visas, auto driving licenses. Also so that they could vote amongst other reasons. They have gone so far as to use the names of dead persons (after checking the death records, then obtaining the birth certificate of the deceased).

As I write, I have my husband's birth certificate and his birth registration in front of me. The birth certificate shows his birth hour. The birth registration does not. This differentiation between a birth certificate and a birth registration is of significant concern to astrologers and updates the material presented in my book *Astrologers Question Box*, No. 16.[2]

Some astrologers insist that their clients obtain a copy of their birth certificates themselves for two reasons: To avoid a delay if only the native, himself, is allowed to procure his own birth certificate, and to receive officially recorded birth data upon which to base the consultation.

However, this may preclude many potential clients who do not have recorded data, or only a relative's word for the birth time. This requirement of the client providing a birth certificate before the work is started could limit an astrologer's business considerably.

Release Form

In Chapter 4 the wording for one release form was given. However, it was suggested that you put the information into your own words to

[1]American Federation of Astrologers, Tempe, AZ [2]AFA, Tempe, AZ

reflect your individual style and personality. Here is how one of my colleagues did so:

> "I, the undersigned, recognize and accept that the analysis of my astrological chart by Chris M. Lenz, MPAI, is done solely in accord with established astrological principles and that this analysis in no way attempts to predict specific future events or to do any other type of fortunetelling."

____

(signed) (date)

Where To Go For Help

There are many state and county agencies, as well as privately owned and operated organizations that offer help, giving specialized services. A handy list of these support groups will allow you to give on-the-spot recommendations to help your clients.

These may include those for children, youth and geriatric populations. Aside from mental health centers, which provide inpatient and outpatient care, precare and aftercare, training and education, other agencies deal with special problems, including drug abuse, mental retardation, spouse abuse and rape. In addition, there are legal services, insurance programs, health systems, accounting services, and the like.

Your local Chamber of Commerce can direct you to where you may obtain one of these referral guides. Or, you can design one yourself from the information given in the telephone book. In any case, because of the many changes which develop in programs responsive to shifting community needs, this guide should be updated periodically. Keep these hotlines current.

Case History

The questionnaire referred to in Chapter 3 and 11 from which to form the case history of a client can be any length. The extent of information rests upon what the client desires from the reading.

For instance, if the information is to be gained from a horary chart, all of the questions will refer to things directly associated with the chief subject matter. In the case of health problems, we would not need to seek a detailed vocational history, even though the onset of an illness may have occurred on the job.

However, instances where the astrologer is considering all of the departments of life to study the past conditioning, or when he is testing a trial chart rectifying the birth time, an extensive questionnaire like the following is useful.

Questionnaire

INSTRUCTIONS: Answer as many questions as you can giving as many details as is possible. Omit only those questions which do not apply to you. If the space following a question is not large enough, kindly use another sheet of paper for your answers accompanied by the appropriate number. Please give DATES, TIMES AND PLACES as accurately as possible.

Submitted by________________________________ Date________
(name and address)

Name of Client______________________________ Sex________
(kept confidential)

Birth Date________________ Birth Time____________ A.M./P.M.
(month, day and year)

Birth Place____
(town, county, state, country)

If rural community, name of nearest large town________________

Its distance from birth place________Miles; ___________Direction

Personal Nationality____________ How many generations?________

Nationality of ancestors______________________________

Physical description (Include current photograph if possible):
Hair:
Height:
Teeth:
Eyes:
Weight:
Nails:
Skin:
Body characteristics:
Scars, birthmarks, etc.:
Describe walk:
Actions: fast or slow:

1. Is your vitality strong?
2. How would you describe your personality?
3. Was your early childhood happy?
4. Describe your relationship with and give birth data (date, hour and place) of father's mother (paternal grandmother) and mother's father (maternal grandfather).
5. Do you have any congenital impairments?
6. Have you had success in money matters, or suffered financial reverses?
7. What kind of possessions do you gather?
8. How do you care for your possessions?
9. What possessions would you consider yours only (not shared)?
10. What philosophical importance do you attach to money?
11. Are you studious?
12. Did you have difficulty in your early schooling?
13. Do you have difficulty learning now?
14. Describe your interest and ability in education.
15. Are you a graduate of High School, College, or other school?
16. How do you get along with relatives?
17. Do you have a driver's license? Did you ever get a ticket? When and why?
18. Name places, dates, conditions under which trips were taken and events which occurred while enroute.
19. Do you have a pilot's (airplane) license? Any legal trouble with it?

20. Describe your communication abilities.
21. Are you renting your home? How long have you lived there?
22. Describe your home life. Has it been harmonious? Give general surroundings and atmosphere of home briefly.
23. Describe your father and your relationship to him (Physical, mental and emotional).
24. Give as complete birth data (date, hour, place) of father as possible.
25. What success have you had in love?
26. Have your sexual attitudes been changing?
27. How do you rate your sex life on a scale from 1 to 10?
28. Do you have a satisfactory sex life?
29. What have been the great emotional periods in your life? Give dates and conditions of these periods.
30. How many children do you have? Give complete birth data (date, time, place) of your children and grandchildren.
31. How do you get along with your children?
32. What is your favorite color? If more than one, please give order of preference.
33. Do you dislike any color? If so, was there something discordant in the past associated with that color? Has your color preference changed since childhood?
34. What is your favorite hobby? Others?
35. What is your attitude toward and your level of participation in sports?
36. Describe your interests and abilities in speculation, gambling, and entertaining.
37. What are your favorite foods?
38. Do any foods disagree with you? Have you suffered from food poisoning? Please give dates.
39. Do you like pets? What kind?
40. What kind of illnesses have you had? How serious were they? Please give dates, using an extra sheet and giving as many details as possible.
41. Accidents? (Please give all types, dates and conditions.)
42. How do you do your work?
43. Do you get along with co-workers?

44. Do you habitually finish the things you start?
45. Have you served in the armed forces? Please give dates of entry and discharge.
46. What is your approach toward health maintainance?
47. What is your approach to problem solving?
48. If married, is your marriage happy? Please describe your marital relationship. Give marriage date, place and time.
49. What is your mate's complete birth data (date, place, time)?
50. What are you looking for in a close relationship?
51. If you are in a business partnership, please describe your relationship and your partner.
52. Please give your business partner's complete birth data (date, place, time).
53. If you are divorced, please give, dates, conditions and reasons.
54. Have you suffered from partners, open enemies, or law suits? If so, please give dates and explain why.
55. What is your relationship with your grandmother on your mother's side? Please give her birth data (date, place, time). What is your relationship with your grandfather on your father's side? Please give his birth data (date, place, time).
56. Please give dates and circumstances of death among family, friends, pets, etc. What effect have they had upon you?
57. Have debts played an important role in your life?
58. Have you been approached many times to lend money? Do you lend money?
59. Have you tried to borrow money often? Do you get it?
60. Have you ever done any banking? Have you handled money for others?
61. Have you had any psychic experiences such as ESP, deja vu, prophetic dreams, mental telepathy, etc.? If so, please describe them and give dates when they occurred.
62. What is the nature of your religion and its meaning to you?
63. Regarding philosophy, do you practice what you preach?
64. Describe your basic philosophy.
65. Have you appeared in court? If so, please explain, give outcome and dates.

66. Have you been published? Books, magazines, etc.? Please give type and dates.
67. What is your occupation? Are you successful?
68. What other occupations have you followed? Have they been successful?
69. Have you had any jobs with emphasis upon honor rather than wages?
70. What is your position in the community?
71. What honors have you received? Please give types and dates.
72. Do you enter into community activity?
73. Please describe your relationship with your mother and give her birth data (date, time, place).
74. Please describe your attitude toward superiors.
75. Please describe yourself as a figure of authority.
76. What kind of friends do you attract?
77. Have you many friends?
78. Do they help you? Please explain and give dates.
79. Do you have more casual friends than close friends?
80. Please describe your relationship with friends.
81. Are you a joiner of clubs, groups, etc.?
82. If you were given three wishes, what would you wish for?
83. Have you had many sorrows and disappointments? Please explain and give dates.
84. Have you suffered from secret enemies? Please explain and give dates.
85. Have you ever been institutionalized, in a hospital, jail, asylum, sanitarium, etc.? Please explain and give dates.
86. Have you ever worked in such an institution? Please name the type of work and give dates.
87. Have you ever been connected in any other capacity with an institution?
88. Under what circumstances do you seek privacy or seclusion?
89. How do you handle your inner fears?
90. What philanthropical moves have you made? Give dates.

Note: Do you have any special areas of interest and/or specific questions?

A little study shows that these questions in the case history relate to subject matter of the horoscope houses, sequentially from house one through house twelve.

Ethics

An important subject—a code of ethics—forms the base of all astrological associations. Most of them include the same ideas even though the words may be a bit different. As an example of such, here's one from the Professional Astrologers Incorporated:

CANONS OF ETHICS

A CONDITION OF MEMBERSHIP is to agree to abide by the following rules of professional conduct and faithfully to discharge the duties of an astrologer, as set forth in the Canon of Ethics of PROFESSIONAL ASTROLOGERS INCORPORATED.

I

It is the duty of an astrologer:

(a) To acknowledge, defend, preserve and cherish the right of every individual to hold, disseminate, and practice whatsoever beliefs he will, and in any manner which is not wrongful.

(b) To maintain inviolate the confidence of a client.

(c) To preserve, even at his peril, those secrets of a client not freely disclosed to him but which he has uncovered in the course of analysis or synthesis of astrological data.

(d) Never to withhold his services from any motive of unreasonable or unworthy personal consideration; contrariwise, never to render service to, inform, or advise a client where the performance of same would rest, wholly or in part, upon privileged information, confidences, or secrets of another client, though not revealed in any way, and which would benefit the one client to the detriment of the other, or comfort the one to the discomfiture of the other, or unfairly affect any relationship whatever between them.

(e) When his circumstances permit, gladly to serve, assist, or counsel, without recompense, those who have neither the monetary nor inner resources to fend off pain or despair.

II

No member of PROFESSIONAL ASTROLOGERS INCORPORATED shall:

(a) Advertise for solicitation of clients, or any other purpose, in a manner which is sensational, or which glorifies his intellect and educational equipment, talents, and accomplishments, or which recounts his past triumphs of prediction, or which features a roster of celebrated or notorious clients and dwells upon their fondness for and reliance upon him, or which proclaims him to be the superior of his fellow Astrologers, or which does not meet with the requirements of dignity and good taste.

(b) Refer to his membership in PROFESSIONAL ASTROLOGERS INCORPORATED in phone listings, advertising, business cards, letterheads, and the like, other than in the following phrase, not unduly emphasized: "Member, P.A.I." or "Member, Professional Astrologers Incorporated."

(c) Disparage a colleague in the hearing of a lay person, or ridicule before the general public theoretical positions, or those who assume them, contrary to his own; contrariwise, no member shall remain silent, or hold his peace, merely to suit his convenience, when astrology is subjected to unfounded accusation or unwarranted attack.

(d) Dispense advice which, under similar circumstances, he would not apply to himself.

(e) Conduct either his professional or personal life in a manner which is so openly haphazard as to call into question the validity of the science and art of Astrology, or conduct himself in any manner which would degrade it or shame his colleagues.

Some years ago in the *American Astrology* magazine (November, 1982) a reader asked about the law requesting information about astrologer's client. The following thoughtful answer appeared:

> "An astrologer asked by law enforcement officials for information on a client would be in a tough predicament. No one wants to be in the position of being asked to violate a client's confidence, but an astrologer has neither the kind of standing before the law that, say, doctors or lawyers do, nor any kind of dedicated professional organization to back him up if he wants to make a legal stand. Refusing to give such information can result in something as "simple" as an indefinite stay in jail for contempt of court or as tough as a felony conviction for charges such as obstruction of justice. Considering the tenuousness of local laws relating to the practice of astrology, any such action by the legal establishment could easily result in the removal of the astrologer's legal right to practice, at the very least."

Both the AFA and the PAI are non-profit organizations and cannot engage in political activities such as defending an astrologer who is cited by the bunco squad for practicing astrology where it is prohibited by law. Basically, it is each astrologer's responsibility to investigate that law before he starts to practice.

However, there is nothing to prevent a non-profit organization from acting as an advisor to a group trying to place a fair astrology ordinance on the books.

Be A Business Leader

Here is a brief resume of what it takes to run your own business. You should know how to handle:

A) Employee relations—hiring, firing, wages and benefits, training.

B) Business methods—records, files maintainance, equipment.

C) Protection-obeying laws, providing safety for workers, having a lawyer to turn to, having property and liability insurance.

D) Money—where and how to get new capital and loans projecting money needs, handling receivables and collections, getting credit from suppliers.

E) Accounting—making financial statement analysis, fitting the system to the business.

F) Business relations—with staff and employees, suppliers, customers, business neighbors, the trade, community.

G) Information sources—trade publications and associations, suppliers, government agencies, educational institutions, libraries, general reading.

In addition to this know-how, a good business person needs to know how to use that information. The Bank of America compiled the following after studying what is required to insure success in a small business.

A business leader is a doer, he:

1) Makes plans, by gathering information, co-ordinating the information, establishing objectives—especially profit goals—and by making initial decisions.

2) Gets action, by setting up an organization, staffing it with people, telling the staff what is to be expected, making them feel like doing their best, giving them orders and supervision, providing them with incentives.

3) Directs the business, by continuously guiding and counseling the staff, measuring results in every way, making new decisions to keep on the right track.

4) Promotes business growth, by developing people, developing new ideas, developing new sources of assistance, expanding into promising new fields.

5) Prepares for the future, by recognizing times change and people grow older, thinking of personal family and estate problems, providing new management for the business, planning in every way possible for the future.

Other actions which tend to spell success for the small business person are when he:

A) Plans the wisest use of business, family and personal time.
B) Sets definite personal and business goals.
C) Puts most plans and policies down in writing.
D) Makes firm decisions after careful thought.
E) Analyzes new and re-analyzes old situations.

F) Persists with an action as long as it is profitable.

G) Ends an action, changes plans, or admits mistakes when things are not working out as planned.

Chase Revel, director of International Entrepreneurs Association—a California based group that helps people get into business by providing manuals on the nation's hottest business projects—summed it up when he said: "It is essential for anyone starting out to have at least a rudimentary knowledge of accounting, advertising, promotion and the technical aspects of the business."

It's Okay to Start Small

Again it is advantageous to remind the would-be professional that he does not need all of the equipment and paraphenalia to set up a business. It is okay to start small and grow from there.

When entrepreneur Revel expanded his remarks, he added. "You don't have to be an expert, but you have to know basically how things work." He added that the difference between success and failure comes down to your own "determination, drive and creativity."

The Gallo brothers were great examples of starting small and growing. They used their determination, drive and creativity to start a business, which eventually became one of the largest enterprises in California. They made sure of their financing and knowledge by educating themselves fully for their new venture.

In 1933, when Prohibition had ended (and there was an experiment that really FAILED!), the Gallo brothers planned to go into wine making. They went to the Modesto Public Library and *researched* the process of making wine and emerged with a recipe.

Then they pooled their resources and came up with $5,900.23 (a considerable amount of money at the end of the Great Depresssion), to use in financing their project. This gave them not only monetary security, but peace of mind to work together without worry over money.

Thus their original *research* and *financing* has turned into an internationally renowned privately family-owned company noted for its consistent quality of product. In slightly more than 50 years, E and J Gallo has grown to a production of 140 million gallons of wine earning some $600 million, providing over one-quarter of the wine sold in the United States annually.

Do you see what careful planning BEFORE you take the giant step into business can provide? E and J Gallo and its various subsidiaries is estimated to be worth close to a billion dollars, not a bad return on a $6,000 investment in 50 years.

Client Records

A manual of this sort would be incomplete without a reference for keeping track of each and every step in serving your client. The following example of a work-in-progress tickler sheet should give you some ideas for designing your own.

Work-In-Progress Tickler Sheet

Name of Client	1	2	3	4	5	6	7	8	9	10
Public, John Q.	5/4	$75.	Natal & Pro.	5/7	5/10	5/11	5/25	10a	—	—
Doe, Mary Jane	5/5	$50.	Prog. Update	5/7	5/10	5/13	—	—	5/14	—

Dates and amounts are entered in these columns, the numbered headings stand for:

1) Order received.
2) Amount paid.
3) Services ordered.

4) Sent to computer.
5) Returned from computer.
6) Preparation completed.
7) Appointment date.
8) Appointment time.
9) Tape mailed.
10) Amount due. (This column should never be used, if possible. It only creates potential difficulties.)

Finally

Remember, the most effective advertising is by word of mouth. What does that depend upon? You! Your thoughts, feelings and actions, and how you conduct and handle your business. Good luck!

ASTROLOGY AS A BUSINESS

There are many who can describe an astrologer's business, but only a rare one can provide the direct experience. Doris Chase Doane does just that.

No wonder this book is a best seller in its field. It tells it like it is—the who, what, where, and how of establishing and building an astrological practice.

Here is a how-to manual with everything from legal requirements to the design of work space. Following these guidelines will enable counselors in this field to raise astrology to its rightful place—that of presenting a professional image to the community.